Consider It All Joy

Forward

This book is written from a Christian point of view, and it is all about the experience of Life being the grandest opportunity for knowing Joy. It is time to see life as a gift and make the most of it. It is time to move through our sorrows, beyond our sufferings, and on to accepting our contentment.

This book walks you into knowing that you choose the love of life every time you choose joy. When you are grateful for your life, you receive satisfaction and joy. I liken it to yoga, in which you learn to be steadfast and maintain a pose. Once you experience several seconds in holding your core muscles together, fight the desire to move about as your mind thinks of everything that comes across it, you come out grateful that you held the pose and do so because someone showed you the actions to take and then supported you in staying to the task.

I would also like you to liken the gift of joy to the gift of grace, for it is a gift given by God.

Acknowledgments

We would like to thank our spouses and family for our space in writing this book. We so much want to bring happiness to humanity. We want to thank Stephanie C. Reaves from Reaves Between the Lines, whose editing and input helped us complete this work. Moreover, we thank God for divine inspiration.

Introduction

What if I told you that if you consider all in life joy, you will find no real reason to feel sorrow as we know it. If you truly apply the message outlined in the blueprints given in life, we can overcome so much pain. We have been allowed to live extraordinary joyful lives, and we have been given the playbook and didn't realize it until now. Suppose we assume that the majority of humanity has not read the Bible; this is now your chance to start. We will start now with the book of St. James.

The book of St. James found in the new testament explains it all; it tells it like it is. We invite you to use your senses to arm yourselves with clarity with each verse read; every reflection you write, you will begin to embody the sensation of healing as you embark on this 40-day journey overdue for you at this very moment.

Why a 40-day journal? Jesus spent 40-days in the desert. Hit the reset button on your life. Embody the changes needed and progress to the next level for the rest of your life.

Read and embrace it all with an open mind. Accept life as it is, for each moment is perfect; all you need is to adjust your lens.

Instructions to adjust your lens

Every day you will be asked to adjust your lens, which is necessary to achieve joy and maintain it. The following are the essential instructions you need to use while on your journey.

Move "FORWARD" from yesterday.

"READ" the verse provided on this new day.

"REFLECT" on words read by writing how it connects to you either by experience or through thoughts of hopes in the future to come.

"READ" your reflection to gain understanding in self.

"REFLECT" on how this more profound connection to your being or knowledge of self is freeing. Listen to your inner spirit.

"READ" the provided verse again with a newfound joy in your heart and peace in your spirit.

40-day reflection

40-day retreat

40-day journey

40-day feat

40-day marathon

40-days to destroy

all negative self-conviction during a 40-day soul cleanse and

Consider It All Joy

Step I

James, New American Standard Bible (NASB)

Testing Your Faith

James, a bond-servant of God and of the Lord Jesus Christ, To the twelve tribes who are dispersed abroad: Greetings. (James 1:1)

DAY 1

Consider it all joy, my brethren, when you encounter various trials, knowing that the testing of your faith produces endurance. And let endurance have its perfect result so that you may be perfect and complete, lacking in nothing. *(James 1:2-4)*

You have joy available to you right now. Even if you are experiencing any type of trouble, joy can be yours. It is all based on what you are looking at, how you are looking at it, and who you say you are.

Why not say who you are with an affirmation? Let's be like Jesus with this one. Jesus said: "I am the way, the truth, and the life." Think about it, and you can declare who you are. Say affirming statements about yourself. Tell yourself the truth in just the way you desire and need to hear it. Maybe you could say: I am awesome, I am grateful, I am patient, I am a good listener, I am the foundation for my family.

Let's celebrate who we are and how we became who we are. Let's answer the questions: Who are you? What makes you smile? What do you like? What are you good at? and finally...WHO ARE YOU?

Please take seven minutes to write your response and confirm your joy in this day by reciting today's affirmation.

Today's affirmation...

I consider it all joy that I am wonderfully made.

DAY 2

But if any of you lacks wisdom, let him ask of God, who gives to all generously and without reproach, and it will be given to him. But he must ask in faith without any doubting, for the one who doubts is like the surf of the sea, driven and tossed by the wind. For that man ought not to expect that he will receive anything from the Lord, being a double-minded man, unstable in all his ways. *(James 1: 5-8)*

Where do you go when you need help when you seek advice? Do you go to people who know you? More times than not, we seek advice from others who are not like-minded with us. People do not see us unless we reveal the real us to them. God does see us. God wants us to be happy. God wants us to believe in what we cannot see. God wants us to make an appointment with him to sit and receive divine inspiration to sit in silence and receive divine inspiration. Go to God, ask God, and be firm.

Stand firm in what you ask God for. What are you asking God for? Don't dance around it, and don't make less of it. Whatever is important to you is important to you. (It may help to talk your ideas over with a loved one.) Please take seven minutes to write your response and confirm your joy in this day by reciting today's affirmation.

Today's affirmation...

I consider it all joy that I am Wisdom.

DAY 3

But the brother of humble circumstances is to glory in his high position, and the rich man is to glory in his humiliation, because like flowering grass, he will pass away. For the sun rises with a scorching wind and withers the grass, and its flower falls off, and the beauty of its appearance is destroyed; so too the rich man in the midst of his pursuits will fade away. *(James 1:9-11)*

Life is full of humbling experiences. Sometimes it is hard to look at what resulted in us experiencing humility. Search your memory and look for an event that resulted in your humbling. Keep in mind being humble is a good thing; it keeps you close to joy. A humble man is a blessed man, for the ego is in check and instead of easing God out, you embrace God more.

How do you experience life? What has humbled you? Did you have an experience that felt uncomfortable and then somehow resulted in a happy experience? Please share from your experiences the joy after the humility:

Please take seven minutes to write your response and confirm your joy in this day by reciting today's affirmation.

Today's affirmation...

I consider it all joy that I am humble.

DAY 4

Blessed is a man who perseveres under trial; for once he has been approved, he will receive the crown of life which the Lord has promised to those who love Him.
(James 1:12)

To persevere under trial, you need to forgive those who put you on trial. Send love to those who placed you there instead. Take a stand. When you stand firm in your belief, you give birth to perseverance. Perseverance born out of faith shapes the humble man which is the beginning of how joy is born.

Many times people talk about being a gracious giver. What about being a gracious receiver? Can we see beyond the humility of receiving and just experience the joy?

It is absolutely okay to be glad in all you have (or to show gratitude for gifts received that only thought existed in your dreams! Write about a time you were thrilled to have experienced the gift of receiving.

Write about what it feels like to receive the desired gift with grace.

Please take seven minutes to write your response and confirm your joy in this day by reciting today's affirmation.

Today's affirmation...

I consider it all joy that I am perseverance.

The book of St. James...Journal to Consider it all Joy

DAY 5

Let no one say when he is tempted, "I am being tempted by God," for God cannot be tempted by evil, and He himself does not tempt anyone. But each one is tempted when he is carried away and enticed by his own lust. Then when lust has conceived, it gives birth to sin, and when sin is accomplished, it brings forth death. *(James 1:13-15)*

No one is exempt from temptation. Jesus was in the desert for 40 days; the length of your journey, and he was tempted. When temptation comes, we can ignore it. We can move forward with wisdom knowing we have overcome adversity, or we can continue to be carried away with negativity and die letting our dreams die with it.

Temptation is overcome by redirecting your attention to that which fits in with your goals. Whenever you are tempted, remind yourself of what you want and then choose an action that gets you closer to your goals. Do not be the cause of the death of your dreams and goals. Do not blame God for your lack of integrity. God is good and only good. Dare to dream for yourself.

List your many dreams and goals. Please take seven minutes to write your response and confirm your joy in this day by reciting today's affirmation.

Today's affirmation...

I consider it all joy that the Lord is my strength.

DAY 6

Do not be deceived, my beloved brethren. Every good thing given and every perfect gift is from above, coming down from the Father of lights, with whom there is no variation or shifting shadow. In the exercise of his will, he brought us forth by the word of truth so that we would be a kind of first fruits among His creatures. *(James 1:16-18)*

We are the first fruits made in God's image, and in the exercise of his will. We have free will! We are born of the spoken word and the word of truth in which the truth brings about joy.

What do you bring forth by your word of truth? What are your first fruits? Meaning, what do you bring to life? What brings life to you?

Reflect on your good deeds and words that being of service to others. Write in the space provided how you give others joy in life with your acts of service.

Please take seven minutes to write your response and confirm your joy in this day by reciting today's affirmation.

Today's affirmation...

I consider it all joy that God is good, all the time and so am I.

The book of St. James...Journal to Consider it all Joy

DAY 7

This you know, my beloved brethren. But everyone must be quick to hear, slow to speak, and slow to anger, for the anger of man does not achieve the righteousness of God. Therefore, putting aside all filthiness and all that remains of wickedness, in humility, receive the word implanted, which is able to save your souls. *(James 1:19-21)*

If you do not check yourself, your emotions can pull you further away from your desires. Emotions need to remain positive, and you must stay calm. You must have something that will give you joy in the midst of people being people.

Remain humble yet authentic in all you do. When your thoughts grow in anger, is there a way that you can turn the anger into a work of good? Write down what triggers you and the solutions you are willing to offer yourself. Here is an example: when I am hollered at, I will sing a song.

Please take seven minutes to write your response and confirm your joy in this day by reciting today's affirmation.

Today's affirmation...

I consider it all joy that I am quick to hear and slow to speak.

DAY 8

But prove yourselves doers of the word and not merely hearers who delude themselves. For if anyone is a hearer of the word and not a doer, he is like a man who looks at his natural face in a mirror; for once he has looked at himself and gone away, he has immediately forgotten what kind of person he was. But one who looks intently at the perfect law, the law of liberty, and abides by it, not having become a forgetful hearer but an effectual doer, this man will be blessed in what he does. *(James 1:22-25)*

You are called to face yourself. We have been asking you if you knew who you were. Do you? Do you know your worth, your abilities? The bigger question is, are you aware of your greatness? Are you a robot who moves about, just another cog in a wheel? Can you see the person in the mirror and say yes, this is who I was meant to be with complete integrity? If the response to the last question is no, then, you must begin today!

Focus on who you want to be! Let go of yesterday's triggers. Move forward; do not get stuck. If you focus on the person you desire to be, you do not have to worry about yesterday.

Live today and make certain that your actions support who you say you are. Write down the steps you can do this day and this week that will support who you say you are.

Please take seven minutes to write your response and confirm your joy in this day by reciting today's affirmation.

Today's affirmation...

I consider it all joy that I am a doer.

_____

_____

_____

_____

_____

_____

_____

_____

_____

_____

_____

_____

_____

_____

_____

_____

DAY 9

If anyone thinks himself to be religious and yet does not bridle his tongue but deceives his own heart, this man's religion is worthless. Pure and undefiled religion in the sight of our God and Father is this: to visit orphans and widows in their distress and keep oneself unstained by the world. *(James: 1:26-27)*

The world doesn't need any more hypocrites. As cliche as it may sound, the world needs "Love sweet Love." That is why we are here. We need to heal the world one person at a time.

Doesn't it feel good to do good deeds without boasting, dictating, or gossiping? What good have you done for others? Make a list. If your list does not feel complete, consider making a list of deeds that others have done for you. Then write out an idea of how you can pay it forward.

Please take seven minutes to write your response and confirm your joy in this day by reciting today's affirmation.

Today's affirmation...

I consider it all joy that I have self-control.

STEP 2

James 2 New American Standard Bible (NASB)

The Sin of Partiality

DAY 10

My brethren, do not hold your faith in our glorious Lord Jesus Christ with an attitude of personal favoritism. For if a man comes into your assembly with a gold ring and dressed in fine clothes, and there also comes in a poor man in dirty clothes, and you pay special attention to the one who is wearing the fine clothes, and say, "You sit here in a good place," and you say to the poor man, "You stand over there, or sit down by my footstool," have you not made distinctions among yourselves, and become judges with evil motives? Listen, my beloved brethren: did not God choose the poor of this world to be rich in faith and heirs of the kingdom which He promised to those who love Him? But you have dishonored the poor man. Is it not the rich who oppress you and personally drag you into court? Do they not blaspheme the fair name by which you have been called? *(James 2:1-7)*

In this passage, it is stated very clearly that we are not to judge others. Whether rich or poor, people should not be judged by anything other than their character. This also brings us to consider biases, stereotypes, and preferences. Do you treat people differently based on their status? All people are worthy of compassion, for compassion is equitable.

Name the people who are rich in virtues that you aspire to hold. What are those virtues or the goodness that you see they possess?

Please take seven minutes to write your response and confirm your joy in this day by reciting today's affirmation.

Today's affirmation...

I consider it all joy that I celebrate the virtuous qualities of myself and others.

DAY 11

If, however, you are fulfilling the royal law according to the Scripture, "You shall love your neighbor as yourself," you are doing well. But if you show partiality, you are committing sin and are convicted by the law as transgressors. For whoever keeps the whole law and yet stumbles in one point, he has become guilty of all. For He who said, "Do not commit adultery," also said, "Do not commit murder." Now, if you do not commit adultery but do commit murder, you have become a transgressor of the law. So speak and so act as those who are to be judged by the law of liberty. For judgment will be merciless to one who has shown no mercy; mercy triumphs over judgment. (James 2:8-13)

Stop judging! We can not repeatedly judge ourselves, nor can we keep judging others. How deficient in self-worth are we to judge or act in prejudice of others, forcing a divide in humanity in this most beautifully diverse world? Judging, a little or a lot is still judging. Offer kindness and mercy to yourself and others. How is diversity celebrated in your life?

Please take seven minutes to write your response and confirm your joy in this day by reciting today's affirmation.

Today's affirmation...

I consider it all joy that I am full of compassion and mercy.

DAY 12

What use is it, my brethren, if someone says he has faith, but he has no works? Can that faith save him? If a brother or sister is without clothing and in need of daily food, and one of you says to them, "Go in peace, be warmed and be filled," and yet you do not give them what is necessary for their body, what use is that? Even so, faith, if it has no works, is dead, being by itself. *(James 2:14-17)*

Be Present. Being present is listening, paying attention, and answering the call. When you need to know how to respond to a situation, you must consider what the moment calls for? Words and prayers alone are not always the cure. Are you willing to administer the prescription? Are you willing to treat the need?

Please take a moment to consider how you have been showing up in your community, in your home, in your church, in your workplace, or school environment. Write down what is needed or where you are needed. If you don't know what is needed, think about what the conversations have been like in these places. (For example, if the complaint is that this place is dirty, the need is to find a way to get the place clean. Likewise, if you heard we don't have clean water, we need to find a way to have clean water.)

Please take seven minutes to write your response and confirm your joy in this day by reciting today's affirmation.

The book of St. James...Journal to Consider it all Joy

Today's affirmation...

I consider it all joy that I have faith and good works.

DAY 13

But someone may well say, "You have faith and I have works; show me your faith without the works, and I will show you my faith by my works." *(James 2:18)*

Our actions are an extension of who we are. Do your actions match who you say you are? Take a few moments to identify what inspires your very being, what intuitively calls you into being, and what you can do to nurture that inspiration. Name your goals and the steps you will actively undertake to consummate them.

Be specific by naming real goals and actions that you would like to see happen.

Please take seven minutes to write your response and confirm your joy in this day by reciting today's affirmation.

Today's affirmation...

I consider it all joy that I have been saved, not by works, but grace, so that I might do good works.

DAY 14

You believe that God is one. You do well; the demons also believe and shudder. But are you willing to recognize, you foolish fellow, that faith without works is useless? *(James 2:19-20)*

God is good because God is good! Everything evil and everything good knows that they are rewarded by faith. The gifts; the rewards received are paid in joy. God's grace and mercy given to us are what we need to give to ourselves and others.

It is essential to give all glory to God. It is good to see the awesomeness of the Lord. What does God move you to do? How are you available to God with the gifts he has given you? How are you using the talents that God has gifted you?

Please take seven minutes to write your response and confirm your joy in this day by reciting today's affirmation.

Today's affirmation...

I consider it all joy that I believe in God, and I am a believer.

DAY 15

Was not Abraham, our father, justified by works when he offered up Isaac, his son, on the altar? You see that faith was working with his works, and as a result of the works, faith was perfected; and the Scripture was fulfilled which says, "And Abraham believed God, and it was reckoned to him as righteousness," and he was called the friend of God. You see that a man is justified by works and not by faith alone. *(James 2:21-24)*

What works do you do in your life that reflect your faith? Is there space for the inspired work of God to show up in your actions? God works through you. Are you open to God showing up and working through you?

God is not asking parents to sacrifice their children in this day and age. God gave us the last living sacrifice in Jesus. God believes all of humanity is worth saving. So, what is the ask here? Can you hear the call of God, our father?

Look at society. We need help, and it starts with you. What work can you do for yourself? What works can you do for the good of humanity? Did you know that one smile a day could help not only you but another faithful servant?

Please take seven minutes to write your response and confirm your joy in this day by reciting today's affirmation.

Today's affirmation...

I consider it all joy that I am a friend of God.

DAY 16

In the same way, was not Rahab the harlot also justified by works when she received the messengers and sent them out by another way? For just as the body without the spirit is dead, so also faith without works is dead. *(James 2:25,26)*

Having faith that all things work out well and pouting while doing so means you are responding to something contrary to what you believe. Faith is going through things knowing that all good is the outcome. One must live in faith, considering all joy knowing that it is coming while waiting in faith. For example, we are often told that 'when one door closes, another one opens'. We need to have faith that this is true. We have to open our senses to what has happened knowing all good things come out of adversity. Consider all things joy with a lively spirit and accept with joy knowing things are done for not only your own good but also for the good of all humanity.

Sometimes we have to listen beyond what the situation is showing us. What is this situation teaching me? What am I to learn from this experience? Write about a time you intuitively knew what to do. This is about listening to your gut.

Please take seven minutes to write your response and confirm your joy in this day by reciting today's affirmation.

Today's affirmation...

I consider it all joy that I listen and make the right choices.

Step 3

James 3 New American Standard Bible (NASB)

The Tongue Is a Fire

DAY 17

Let not many of you become teachers, my brethren, knowing that as such, we will incur a stricter judgment, for we all stumble in many ways. If anyone does not stumble in what he says, he is a perfect man, able to bridle the whole body as well. Now, if we put the bits into the horses' mouths so that they will obey us, we direct their entire body as well. *(James 3:1-3)*

We have all been called to lead by example. Elders, mentors, parents, siblings are teachers because life gives them experiences to be shared. When you share with others, know that what you think, say, and do could be under the magnifying glass of the judgemental. Knowing that your every move is watched, you may stumble. When you stumble, you learn. All are role models with one goal in mind; to serve humanity. This world is a lab, our world where we make mistakes and learn from them. We learn from each other. In receiving from acts of kindness given, we give for acts of kindness received.

As teachers we should be ethical beings and worthy of being role models. Our actions, if wrong, could lead someone astray. Let's look at the small things, your everyday task. What do your actions show?

Please take seven minutes to write your response and confirm your joy in this day by reciting today's affirmation.

Today's affirmation...

I consider it all joy that I have self-control.

DAY 18

Look at the ships also, though they are so great and are driven by strong winds, are still directed by a very small rudder wherever the inclination of the pilot desires. So also, the tongue is a small part of the body, and yet it boasts of great things. *(James 3:4-5)*

Please take seven minutes to write your responses and confirm your joy in this day by reciting today's affirmation.

Today's affirmation...

I consider it all joy that I control my thoughts and my words.

Part 1 *Do you know the power of the words you speak? Give an example of when you said encouraging words to someone that made them change their direction.*

_____

_____

_____

_____

_____

_____

_____

_____

_____

_____

_____

_____

_____

Part 2 *If you could speak words to help someone go in the right direction, what would they be?*

_____

_____

_____

_____

_____

_____

_____

_____

_____

_____

_____

_____

_____

DAY 19

See how great a forest is set aflame by such a small fire! And the tongue is a fire, the very world of iniquity; the tongue is set among our members as that which defiles the entire body, and sets on fire the course of our life, and is set on fire by hell. (James 3:5b,6)

A fire's blaze will burn to destroy or shine a light to that which is dark. What fire do you seek to fuel with your self-talk? Will you choose to eradicate or illuminate the greatness that occupies your being?

Today would be an excellent time for you to remind yourself how amazing you are. Write down your amazing attributes. You are unique and have so many. Write them down and claim who you are!

Please take seven minutes to write your response and confirm your joy in this day by reciting today's affirmation.

Today's affirmation...

I consider it all joy that I speak exciting words of great energy.

DAY 20

For every species of beasts and birds, of reptiles and creatures of the sea, is tamed and has been tamed by the human race. *(James 3:7)*

If we can tame any and everything, why is it difficult for us humans to tame our own thoughts? We must learn to govern ourselves, our thoughts, and our words.

Please take seven minutes to write your responses and confirm your joy in this day by reciting today's affirmation.

Today's affirmation...

I consider it all joy that I am a powerful being.

Part 1 *Write down the words and thoughts that take residence in you.*

_____

_____

_____

_____

_____

_____

Part 2 Rewrite those words with a positive spin. Think about a loss or upset. Write down, "I look forward to when I experience relief from that loss or upset."

_____

_____

_____

_____

_____

_____

_____

_____

_____

_____

_____

DAY 21

But no one can tame the tongue; it is a restless evil and full of deadly poison. With it, we bless our Lord and Father, and with it, we curse men, who have been made in the likeness of God; from the same mouth come both blessing and cursing. My brethren, these things ought not to be this way. *(James 3:8-10)*

Please consider this passage and reflect, "But the Lord stood by me and gave me strength so that through me the proclamation might be completed and all the Gentiles might hear it. And I was rescued from the lion's mouth." 2 Timothy 4:17

Can you recall a time when your words gave life to something inspired? Write it down, and then express how it made you feel.

Please take seven minutes to write your response and confirm your joy in this day by reciting today's affirmation.

Today's affirmation...

I consider it all joy that the fruit I produce brings great joy to God.

DAY 22

Does a fountain send out from the same opening both fresh and bitter water? *(James 3:11)*

You should not mix dirty and filtered water in your cup and claim it is filtered for drinking. Do your very own thoughts and words repel each other? You know that does not work. You can not hold thoughts of disapproval and love for yourself in the same thought. Opposing views compete for your energy and become a misrepresentation of who you truly are in the world. Choose your position and stand firm in it. Write down all of the ways that you are a loving shield of God with yourself while excluding written attributes of disdain.

Please take seven minutes to write your response and confirm your joy in this day by reciting today's affirmation.

Today's affirmation...

I consider it all joy that I am confident.

The book of St. James...Journal to Consider it all Joy

DAY 23

Can a fig tree, my brethren, produce olives, or a vine produce figs? Nor can salt water produce fresh. *(James 3:12)*

Just as things can only produce what they are made to produce, humans can only produce that which they think to produce. Look at the inventions of man. Before there was a car, it was a thought, and before there was a wheel, it was a thought. The French philosopher René Descartes's statement "I think, therefore, I am" can be implied that as a human thinks they are, they are.

When you think of your future, you must think only of the good you wish to see and experience. Write down the thoughts you should cling to in order to attain the prosperous future you want.

Please take seven minutes to write your response and confirm your joy in this day by reciting today's affirmation.

Today's affirmation...

I consider it all joy that I deserve all the good things that life has to offer.

DAY 24

Who among you is wise and understanding? Let him show by his good behavior his deeds in the gentleness of wisdom. But if you have bitter jealousy and selfish ambition in your heart, do not be arrogant and so lie against the truth. *(James 3:13-14)*

What would a wise person do?

We should be careful not to have an agenda when performing good deeds. We should do good deeds because we do good deeds for joy. Good deeds are for love and not for ambition. Make a list of good doings. The list can be of things you have done or would like to do.

Please take seven minutes to write your response and confirm your joy in this day by reciting today's affirmation.

Today's affirmation...

I consider it all joy that I am doing good things.

DAY 25

This wisdom is not that which comes down from above but is earthly, natural, demonic. For where jealousy and selfish ambition exist, there is disorder and every evil thing. *(James 3:15-16)*

Earthly disorder, chaos, and confusion are not of God. When disorder occurs, we speak words of order that are of God to restore it to its proper way of being. Shake off the dust and disorder of this world. Put on your full armor of God.

Consider a time when you were tasked with the restoration of a relationship. Write about your experience and remember how you felt once it was restored.

Please take seven minutes to write your response and confirm your joy in this day by reciting today's affirmation.

Today's affirmation...

I consider it all joy that I focus on the positive.

DAY 26

But the wisdom from above is first pure, then peaceable, gentle, reasonable, full of mercy and good fruits, unwavering, without hypocrisy. *(James 3:17)*

Most of us desire to know the truth; however, the truth does not always leave us comfortable as we are often unable to accept it as it is. What personal truth do you bury? Through which lens are you viewing it? Write about this truth in a way that allows you to experience reasonableness and peace.

Please take seven minutes to write your response and confirm your joy in this day by reciting today's affirmation.

Today's affirmation...

I consider it all joy that I have health and abundance.

DAY 27

And the seed whose fruit is righteousness is sown in peace by those who make peace. *(James 3:18)*

Forgiveness is the seed of the righteous. Love is the seed of the righteous.

When you do an action that is good because the thought and intention of it are good, expect good things to come. Write new endings for your stories now. Dream big and write.

Know this, you cannot change what has already occurred but you have the power to control your thoughts right here and right now. "Nothing changes until you change it," Pastor Paul Andell, St. James Lutheran Church, Philadelphia.

Please take seven minutes to write your response and confirm your joy in this day by reciting today's affirmation.

Today's affirmation...

I consider it all joy that I am a peacemaker.

Step 4

James 4 New American Standard Bible (NASB)

Things to Avoid

DAY 28

What is the source of quarrels and conflicts among you? Is not the source of your pleasures that wage war in your members? You lust and do not have, so you commit murder. You are envious and cannot obtain, so you fight and quarrel. You do not have because you do not ask. You ask and do not receive because you ask with wrong motives so that you may spend it on your pleasures. You adulteresses, do you not know that friendship with the world is hostility toward God? Therefore whoever wishes to be a friend of the world makes himself an enemy of God. Or do you think that the Scripture speaks to no purpose: "He jealously desires the Spirit which He has made to dwell in us"? (James 4:1-5)

We have all lived and taken part as people in this world who fought, were jealous, and did things with wrong motives. Whatever your intentions, I hope they are good. You accept the lessons learned in life and consider it all joy with good intentions.

Imagine speaking to God while he is reading your true intentions. Do you tell God what you really want? Expose yourself as if he already knows who you are.

Write a love letter to God. Let God know where you stand in the relationship and then tell him what you want.

Please take seven minutes to write your response and confirm your joy in this day by reciting today's affirmation.

Today's affirmation...

I consider it all joy that I ask and I receive because I have a pure heart.

DAY 29

But He gives a greater grace. Therefore it says, "God is opposed to the proud, but gives grace to the humble." Submit therefore to God. Resist the devil and he will flee from you. Draw near to God and He will draw near to you. Cleanse your hands, you sinners; and purify your hearts, you double-minded. Be miserable and mourn and weep; let your laughter be turned into mourning and your joy to gloom. Humble yourselves in the presence of the Lord, and He will exalt you. (James 4:6-10)

Remember that you are a gift. A gift of life that thrives in experiencing that which lives. The uniqueness of your very being is such a gift as all that you are is because God is. Write down all that God has given you. Do not be modest as here you will find what humbles you. Remember, you are not entitled to what it is that you do have and cherish.

Please take seven minutes to write your response and confirm your joy in this day by reciting today's affirmation.

Today's affirmation...

I consider it all joy that I draw near to God and He draws near to me.

DAY 30

Do not speak against one another, brethren. He who speaks against a brother or judges his brother, speaks against the law and judges the law; but if you judge the law, you are not a doer of the law but a judge of it. There is only one Lawgiver and Judge, the One who is able to save and to destroy, but who are you who judge your neighbor? *James 4:11-12)*

Forgive us our trespasses and we forgive those who trespass against us. We must do this for in forgiveness we are restored. In forgiveness we have joy and if we consider everything joy there is no point in ever lowering yourself to someone else's standards. Instead of judging your neighbor, love them and then you will be aligned with the one who is able to save and you will save yourself in return.

We have been given the chance to love one another. When you love yourself and others completely, there isn't room for judgment. Who is the last person that you criticized or spoke of with disfavor? Write a letter that does not condemn but is filled with love to this person.

Please take seven minutes to write your response and confirm your joy in this day by reciting today's affirmation.

Today's affirmation...

I consider it all joy that *my kind words are sweet to the* *soul and healing to the bones of others.*

DAY 31

Come now, you who say, "Today or tomorrow we will go to such and such a city, and spend a year there and engage in business and make a profit." Yet you do not know what your life will be like tomorrow. You are just a vapor that appears for a little while and then vanishes away. Instead, you ought to say, "If the Lord wills, we will live and also do this or that." But as it is, you boast in your arrogance; all such boasting is evil. Therefore, to one who knows the right thing to do and does not do it, to him, it is sin. *James 4:13-17*

Every day is a blessing from God. We know that tomorrow is not promised. Do not permit another day to go by without expressing your gratitude for the one before you; for we know each consecutive one isn't guaranteed. Write a daily prayer that expresses gratitude for your life.

Please take seven minutes to write your response and confirm your joy in this day by reciting today's affirmation.

Today's affirmation...

I consider it all joy that in God I live.

Step 5

James 5 New American Standard Bible (NASB)

Misuse of Riches

DAY 32

Come now, you rich, weep and howl for your miseries which are coming upon you. Your riches have rotted and your garments have become moth-eaten. Your gold and your silver have rusted, and their rust will be a witness against you and will consume your flesh like fire. It is in the last days that you have stored up your treasure! Behold, the pay of the laborers who mowed your fields, and which has been withheld by you, cries out against you; and the outcry of those who did the harvesting has reached the ears of the Lord of Sabaoth. You have lived luxuriously on the earth and led a life of wanton pleasure; you have fattened your hearts in a day of slaughter. *(James: 5:1-5)*

Look at who you are. The amazing person that you are. You might have demons, problems, or a past experience that bothers you. Look without fear and face it. Face any wrongs you have done as you can not make it better if you keep your eyes closed.

No matter what you have done, as long as you have breath, you have time to reform and face the ghosts of your wrongdoings. What do you need to be made anew? Acknowledge it and write it down alongside a plan of restoration. Make certain to draw a line through the past that you've acknowledged in your writing and say goodbye.

Give this gift to yourself. Right, your wrongs by writing them out with a happy ending based on your good intentions.

Please take seven minutes to write your response and confirm your joy in this day by reciting today's affirmation.

Today's affirmation...

I consider it all joy that God does not look at my outward appearance. He looks at my heart, and he knows my soul.

DAY 33

You have condemned and put to death the righteous man; he does not resist you. *(James: 5:6)*

Just as Jesus was condemned and put to death we perpetuate that when we condemn ourselves. You have condemned a righteous man when you feed yourself all of the stories that others put into your head. When you fail because you say you are not good enough, you condemn a righteous man. God made all of humanity righteous. We were made in God's image to do great things. When we are told we can't and believe it, we condemn our future. We throw away all that we could have been.

Now is the time that we can restore ourselves. Claim this time for self-restoration. Declare that you are restored.

We sometimes validate wrong actions that we believe are right to us. We do not consider those things that are right unless they are right to us.

I do not want to condemn the righteous man. How can I fix this? How is it that God has stayed with me even when I took part in doing wrong to another person?

For if, while we were God's enemies, we were reconciled to him through the death of his Son, how much more, having been reconciled, shall we be saved through his life! Romans 5:10

Can I give an example? Look at me. I knock myself down even though I am good. I don't acknowledge when I am hurt because I say I was at fault. I might be the righteous man that I am putting to death. To free myself, I had to call on the Lord. I had to choose to no longer condemn. I had to choose to forgive myself for not loving me enough and infecting humanity. When you are not who you are supposed to be, you condemn the righteous man. Don't resist yourself, don't resist the real you. You were made in God's image. Look in the mirror and declare your restoration today. "I am restored." Reflect: God wants a relationship with us. Write a letter to God about this.

Please take seven minutes to write your response and confirm your joy in this day by reciting today's affirmation.

Today's affirmation...

I consider it all joy that I am restored, and I could not experience an abundant life except for Jesus and the cross.

DAY 34

Therefore be patient, brethren, until the coming of the Lord. The farmer waits for the precious produce of the soil, being patient about it until it gets the early and late rains. You too be patient; strengthen your hearts, for the coming of the Lord, is near. *(James: 5:7-8)*

The amount of patience one has is unknown until tested. When you give up due to lack of patience, you relinquish the possibilities that could have been awaiting you on the other side of it. Patience is easier to practice when you stand firm in the desired goal. What and who are you practicing patience for?

If you can not see what you are hoping for, it does not mean that it is time to stop; it is simply time to write your desired goal clearly while imagining how attaining it will make you feel. Now let us make this goal into a prayer free from fear. This prayer of the goal must be focused on the joy of what it is to attain.

Please take seven minutes to write your response and confirm your joy in this day by reciting today's affirmation.

Today's affirmation...

I consider it all joy that I wait on the Lord.

DAY 35

Do not complain, brethren, against one another, so that you yourselves may not be judged; behold, the Judge is standing right at the door. *(James: 5:9)*

There is no judgment as grave as the final judgment; so be prudent in your daily affairs to not detract your righteousness. What do others judge you for? Write it down, release it and remember; God knows the desires and intentions of your heart. His final judgment is the only judgment that matters.

Please take seven minutes to write your response and confirm your joy in this day by reciting today's affirmation.

Today's affirmation...

I consider it all joy that I have much to rejoice about.

DAY 36

As an example, brethren, of suffering and patience, take the prophets who spoke in the name of the Lord. We count those blessed who endured. You have heard of the endurance of Job and have seen the outcome of the Lord's dealings, that the Lord is full of compassion and is merciful. (James: 5:10-11)

There must have been a lesson or an affirming thought that you must have to learn, whether it be to forgive others or yourself. Here we are asked to reflect on the story of Job. Had he not remained steadfast to the Lord and practiced patience, all that he received in glory would be inaccessible. So often we give up on patience at the very moment the benefit is to come. What are the benefits that you hope to see? Write it all down.

Please take seven minutes to write your response and confirm your joy in this day by reciting today's affirmation.

Today's affirmation...

I consider it all joy that the Lord is kind and merciful.

DAY 37

But above all, my brethren, do not swear, either by heaven or by earth or with any other oath; but your yes is to be yes, and your no, no, so that you may not fall under judgment. *(James: 5:12)*

Shakespeare would say, "To thine own self be true." Stand up for yourself because you are all you have. You are amazing and need no validation from anyone. You do not have to do anything that you do not want to do. You are your own person.

Be authentic. Be you. Stand in who you are; let your words be a full reflection of your being. Declare who you are and write it down.

Please take seven minutes to write your response and confirm your joy in this day by reciting today's affirmation.

Today's affirmation...

I consider it all joy that I am authentic.

The book of St. James...Journal to Consider it all Joy

DAY 38

Is anyone among you suffering? Then he must pray. Is anyone cheerful? He is to sing praises. Is anyone among you sick? Then he must call for the elders of the church and they are to pray over him, anointing him with oil in the name of the Lord; and the prayer offered in faith will restore the one who is sick, and the Lord will raise him up, and if he has committed sins, they will be forgiven him. *(James: 5:13-15)*

This is called living. In life, we deal with what is presented in the present time. Whichever life moment you find yourself from the list from above, allow yourself to "be" in it. What is the action that this passage is directing you to do in this moment? Write it down.

Please take seven minutes to write your response and confirm your joy in this day by reciting today's affirmation.

Today's affirmation...

I consider it all joy that When I humble myself before God in prayer, he hears me.

DAY 39

Therefore, confess your sins to one another, and pray for one another so that you may be healed. The effective prayer of a righteous man can accomplish much. Elijah was a man with a nature like ours, and he prayed earnestly that it would not rain, and it did not rain on the earth for three years and six months. Then he prayed again, and the sky poured rain and the earth produced its fruit. *(James: 5:16-28)*

What a great being you are! There is so much power in prayer. So humble and yet powerful enough that God can hear you. If you are living in your truth, say a great prayer, give patience and wait. Write down one of your great prayers now.

Please take seven minutes to write your response and confirm your joy in this day by reciting today's affirmation.

Today's affirmation...

I consider it all joy that I pray powerfully.

DAY 40

My brethren, if any among you strays from the truth and one turns him back, let him know that he who turns a sinner from the error of his way will save his soul from death and will cover a multitude of sins. (James: 5:19-20)

This entire journey was our way of helping you turn away from conforming to this world and transforming into who you were meant to be: a person who is full of joy, a person who listens to themselves; fearless.

The gospel song, "If I can help somebody" plays in my head. The lyrics are "If I can help somebody as I travel on, then my living has not been in vain." So this is it. What are you going to do?

Make each day count!

Please take seven minutes to write your responses and confirm your joy in this day by reciting today's affirmation.

Today's affirmation...

I consider it all joy that I have been saved so that I am empowered to do good works for humanity.

Part 1 How are you going to show up for yourself today?

_____

_____

_____

_____

_____

_____

_____

_____

_____

_____

_____

_____

_____

_____

_____

_____

Part 2 With each day forward, how will you diligently act in commitment to showing up for yourself?

_____

_____

_____

The book of St. James...Journal to Consider it all Joy

You have reached the end of your 40-day journal. Remind yourself daily that you are amazing. You started by taking baby steps to become the real you, your authentic self. You must recognize that you feel, know, believe, and declare yourself awesome and worthy of joy. Your joy is yours and everyone around you benefits from it. In order for you to receive your greatness, you must allow your authentic self to come out and embrace the goodness that you always knew you were.

You are called to wake up and put on your new self. Arise from your slumber. We are all meant to live a joy-filled life. We were created for joy; God's joy! God wants us to have joy all day, every day. We are required to if we are to survive this world.

In adversity, find joy. In joy, find life and in everything; find happiness. We have been placed here for joy. Faith and endurance are the benefits of joy. Remain grateful always, and when you are weary, draw upon the wisdom from the most high.

*From this day forward, consider it **ALL JOY**! Your thoughts should always be joyous.*

Release your resistance to be happy!

Barbara Purnell Boyle

Barbara Purnell Boyle has received her MS Church Management from Villanova University and her BA in Speech Communication from Penn State. Barbara is a former Gospel Choir Director, Director of Religious Education, Pastoral Associate for St. Francis of Assisi Church, and a former Director of Youth and Young Adult Ministry at St. Vincent de Paul Church. She has worked as a family and student advisor for an online K-12 school for ten years. She continues to see the value of involving youth in church life. Barbara is married to Charles and they have seven children between them.

Antoinette Marie Reaves

For the past 30 years, she has performed and choreographed liturgical dances for churches in the Germantown/Mt. Airy area. She is an actress/ Singer/ Dancer, co-Founder/and one of the Coordinators of the Immanuel Movement. Her stage credits include Flown, Hecuba, in the Trojan Women, soloist at the Kimmel Center's main stage (through invitation), Chicago where she played June, Children of Eden, The Passion of Christ, Backstage, and Godspell. She stage-managed Bloodknot, Uncle Vanga, and Sound of a Voice. Assistant stage manager in the Passion. Formerly the DRE, Gospel choir director of St. Francis of Assisi Gospel Choir and St. Vincent Depaul of Germantown's Gospel Choir. Former coordinator of the Philadelphia Catholic Mass Choir. Antoinette received her Bachelor of Arts in Human Service from Villanova University. Since she obtained her MA in Theater, she received her MA in Theology from LaSalle University, her MS Educational Leadership/Administrative Certification (PK-12) with Autism Endorsement from Neumann University. Antoinette is currently pursuing her doctorate in Educational Leadership from Liberty University. She is married to Horace W. Reaves; they have one daughter Stephanie and three grandchildren, Kiana, Iryll, and Honor. She is inspired to help humanity reach its fullest potential.

Made in the USA
Middletown, DE
20 February 2023

24525973R00059